"This is an engaging, compelling and accessible book on one of the most significant topics today. John Lennox and Katy Morgan show us that, rather than science discrediting belief in God, belief in God actually provides a reason and motive for science. This is a book which will make all of us think, whether we're scientists, Christians, both or neither. Highly recommended."

SAM ALLBERRY, Author, *Why Does God Care Who I Sleep With?* and *Why Bother with Church?*

"This is the sort of book I wish I'd read as a teenager: a clear, thoughtful and brightly written take on the relationship between Christianity and science. John and Katy don't doesn't duck the tough questions, and they handle them with insight and wit. Bravo."

ANDREW WILSON, Author, *Remaking the World* and *God of All Things*

"Here is crystal clarity on an issue that confuses and deters many would-be believers. This book is so worth reading and passing on to your science-loving friends—whether you or they are a Christian or not."

GLEN SCRIVENER, Author, *The Air We Breathe;* Author and Presenter of 321course.com

SCIENCE AND GOD

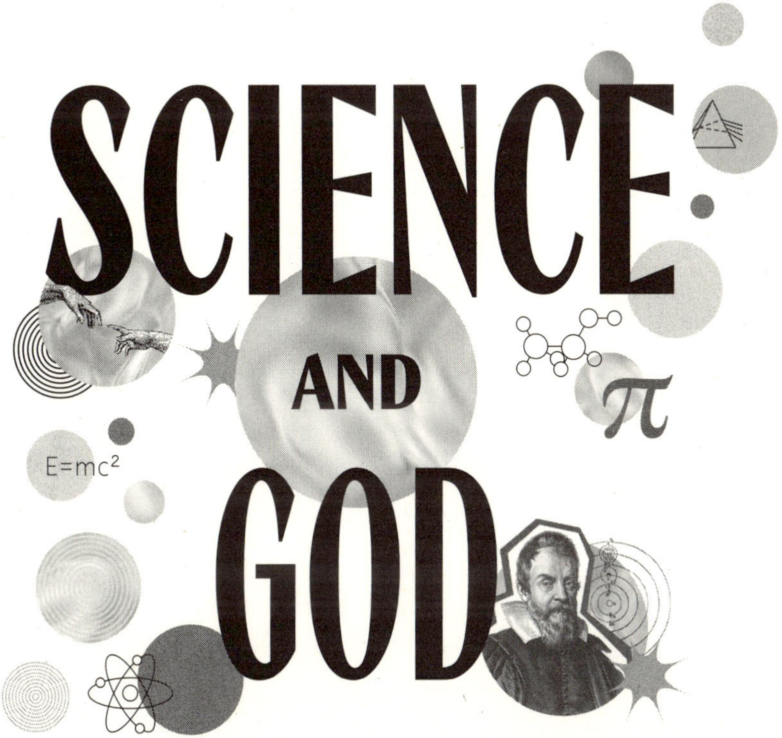

Do You Have to Choose?

JOHN C. LENNOX
KATY MORGAN

Science and God

Published by:
The Good Book Company

thegoodbook.com | thegoodbook.co.uk
thegoodbook.com.au | thegoodbook.co.nz

Every book published by The Good Book Company has been written by human authors and edited by a human editor. While AI tools have been used to assist in the design elements of this book, all content has been created by a human author and thoroughly checked by our editorial team.

Design by Drew McCall

ISBN: 9781802543728 | JOB-008536 | Printed in India

CONTENTS

INTRODUCING THE AUTHORS

Hello, I'm John.

I'm a scientist—a mathematician, to be exact. I am Professor of Mathematics at the University of Oxford, and I've also worked at universities in Wales and Germany. I'm also a Christian, and I've always been interested in the relationship between my passion for science and my faith in God. Ever since I was a teenager (as you'll read about in chapter 1), I've been having conversations with very clever scientists about faith, science and God. I've taken part in big public debates with world-famous atheists like Richard Dawkins and Christopher Hitchens, and I've written several books.

My whole life has been shaped by science, and by my faith in the God of the Bible. To me, the two work perfectly together. But don't just take my word for it—read on!

And I'm Katy.

When I was at school, physics was one of my favourite subjects. But unlike John, I didn't become a scientist. (I actually studied ancient languages at university—a different type of geekery—and now I'm a writer and book editor.) Like John, I am also a Christian, and I've always thought it is important to make sure everyone gets an opportunity to have a proper think about whether God exists, and what he's like if he does.

I spend lots of my spare time volunteering with children and teenagers, and I've written several books for those age groups. When John asked me if I would write this book with him, I was delighted! It was an opportunity for me to learn a lot more about science—but also a chance to help people like you think through some big questions about life, the universe and everything. Which is one of my favourite things to do.

The two of us wrote this book together, but all of the stories and examples come from John. So when you see the word "I", it's John you should imagine!

WHY READ THIS BOOK?

I wonder if you've ever thought much about the universe.

I mean this whole, huge, mind-blowingly enormous, deeply mysterious world.

Did you know that there are more stars in the universe than there are grains of sand on all the beaches on Earth?*

And that an average cloud weighs around a million tonnes?**

And that there's a planet somewhere out there that is mostly made of diamond?***

Thinking about our marvellously mysterious universe is something that two groups of people have in common: scientists and religious people.

You might be used to thinking of scientists and religious people as entirely distinct from one another.

---

* That's at least a billion trillion.

** This is assuming that it is about a kilometre (0.6 miles) high, wide and deep. How can such a heavy object float? It's because a cloud's density (how closely the particles are packed together) is lower than the surrounding air.

*** It's been named 55 Cancri e.

But in reality, scientists and religious people *do* have a lot in common (not least because, sometimes, they're the same person).

They both want to know the truth about the universe. They're both curious about the mysteries of how this world works and how it began. They're both full of wonder at the world around them and excited to find out about it.

Perhaps you are, too?

A lot of people in our world think that you can't believe in God and in science at the same time, and you have to choose between them. Sadly, it's no surprise if you have got the impression that believing in God is a bit old-fashioned and silly—so you don't want to hear about religion or engage with it. It's also no surprise if you've got the opposite idea: you've heard that science could undermine your faith in God, and so you don't want to think about science or engage with it more than you have to.

Or maybe you're not sure what you think about either!

This book is an invitation to be curious, no matter what your current beliefs are. It's an opportunity to engage with *both* science *and* God at the same time, and see what happens. It's a book that, hopefully, will make you more excited about science and more curious about God. Or more curious about science and more excited about God. Or more curious *and* more excited about both—with a dose of wonder thrown in as well.

We'll start by thinking about what science and faith actually *are*—what they're for and why they're important. We'll discover why many scientists do believe in God and think about some of the evidence for the existence of a Creator. Then, starting in chapter 5, we'll look specifically at Christian beliefs about God, the universe and everything. Once again, we'll consider the evidence and come face to face with the most curious questions.

Think of it as an experiment. We're not in a lab, but that doesn't mean we don't have an opportunity to find out something—something that really matters.

So... are you ready to explore the mysteries of the universe?

Chapter 1

THE TROUBLE WITH GALILEO

Can you be a scientist and believe in God?

Galileo Galilei was in serious trouble.

It was 1633, and he was on trial. An astronomer who studied the stars, Galileo had been a bit too noisy about his view that the earth revolves around the sun. (Which, of course, it does—but most people didn't know that at the time.) The Chief Inquisitor of the Roman Catholic Church had forced him into court. And what was the verdict?

Guilty. Or, to use their words:

We pronounce, judge, and declare that you, the said Galileo ... have rendered yourself vehemently suspected by this Holy Office of heresy.

Galileo's ideas about the planets went against the official teaching of the church (which, at the time, said that the sun revolved around the earth). That's what "heresy" means: going against the church. The court banned one of Galileo's books and sent him to prison.

Science and religion were in conflict.

Or... were they?

Do God and Science Mix?

Galileo's story is often mentioned today when people want to say that science and religion are enemies of each other. They say things like this:

> *Galileo was treated appallingly, all because he was brave enough to speak up for scientific truth. The church was obstructing science—and that hasn't stopped. It simply is not possible to be a genuine scientist and a religious believer. God and science just do not work together.*

This sometimes leads to scientists saying things like this:

> The world needs to wake up from the long nightmare of religion. Anything we scientists can do to weaken the hold of religion should be done.

That's a quote from the American theoretical physicist Stephen Weinberg.*

When respected scientists say things like that, many people start to think it must be true that God and science are enemies.

So you might be surprised to learn that Galileo thought they *do* mix! He believed in God and the Bible all his life, both before and after his trial in 1633. To give you an example, he once wrote:

> ***The laws of nature are written by the hand of God in the language of mathematics.***

You might also be surprised to learn that a letter Galileo wrote in 1615 reveals that the debate around his scientific claims didn't start in the church at all. The first people who disagreed with him were other scientists (or natural philosophers, as they were known at the time), and they seem to have persuaded the officials of the church to intervene.** Galileo's theories didn't just contradict the teaching of the church—they contradicted what most other scientists thought. And those scientists didn't like that. (It has to be said that Galileo's talent for irritating people may have had something to do with his arrest, too.)***

* Stephen Weinberg, *New Scientist*, Issue 2578, 18 November 2006.

** Galileo wrote about this in his *Letter to the Grand Duchess Christina*.

*** It's also worth mentioning that, far from being tortured and left to rot in a dirty prison cell, Galileo was allowed to spend his imprisonment in the luxurious houses of his friends. You can see that saying, "Galileo was treated appallingly because he stood up for science against religion" is not actually true!

So this wasn't really a conflict between science and religion. It was a conflict between scientists.

Galileo wasn't alone in being a scientist with religious faith. Look at a list of Nobel Prize winners between 1901 and 2000, for example, and you'll find that more than 60% of them were Christians.* Many scientists have believed in God, throughout history and also in the modern day.

Let's hear from three of them now.

Introducing...

Sir Ghillean Prance is a botanist and ecologist: he studies plants. As well as having been the director of Kew Gardens in London, he has spent time living in the Amazon rainforest, where he identified more than 350 new plant species, and has written about what conservationists can learn from the Amazon tribespeople. He describes his Christian faith this way:**

> For many years I have believed that God is the great designer behind all nature … All my studies in science since then have confirmed my faith.

---

* According to *100 Years of Nobel Prizes* by Baruch Aba Shalev (Atlantic, 2003), 65.4% of Nobel Prize Laureates between 1901 and 2000 have identified Christianity as their religious preference. Overall, Christians have won a total of 78.3% of all the Nobel Prizes in Peace, 72.5% in Chemistry, 65.3% in Physics, 62% in Medicine, 54% in Economics and 49.5% of all Literature awards.

** He wrote this in a booklet called *God and the Scientists,* compiled by Michael Poole in 1997.

Then there's Francis Collins, an expert in genetics who served as the head of the Human Genome Project for many years, and also had a stint as Science Advisor to the President of the USA. Collins played a major role in a huge scientific achievement: mapping the DNA of human beings. He became a Christian in his 20s. Collins once said in a talk:*

> For me, faith [in God] and science always – from the time of my conversion – seemed incredibly complementary … They were two ways of knowing, but knowing different things and asking different questions. Science asking how, faith answering why.

And you may have heard of Rosalind Picard, the inventor and computer scientist whose work at the famous Massachusetts Institute of Technology (MIT) has influenced robotics research, autism research and emotion research. Like Francis Collins, Picard was raised as an atheist

* You can read the whole talk here: biologos.org/personal-stories/is-there-a-god-and-does-he-care-about-me-the-testimony-of-biologos-founder-francis-collins

(not believing in God) but became a Christian as a young adult. She wrote:*

> Both science and religious faith are important parts of the age-old human quest to find out what's true and what's good.

So it seems that science and faith in God *can* mix after all.

But that leaves us with a head-scratcher. Why do some scientists say they *don't*?

No Room for God?

When I was a 19-year-old university student, I once found myself sitting at a dinner next to a Nobel Prize winner. I'd never met such an important scientist before, and I was keen to make the most of the conversation. In particular, I was interested to know what his studies had led him to think about the existence of God. But when I asked about this, he was obviously uncomfortable with the question.

I changed the subject quickly. But after the meal was over, this eminent scientist invited me to come to his study to continue our conversation. There were some other professors there too, but I was the only student.

"Lennox," the Nobel Prize winner said in a forbidding tone, "do you want a career in science?"

"Yes, sir," I replied nervously.

"Then," he told me, "in front of witnesses, tonight,

---

* From *101 Great Big Questions About God and Science*, edited by Lizzie Henderson and Steph Bryant (Lion Hudson, 2022), page 112.

you must give up this childish faith in God. If you do not, then it will cripple you intellectually. You simply won't make it as a scientist."

Talk about pressure!

This highly respected scientist had more or less the same view of things as the physicist I quoted earlier—the one who said that scientists should do anything they can to get people to stop being religious. And there are a lot of scientists out there who think this. They say that Christianity, and religion generally, is fundamentally opposed to the practice of science. They say that science leaves no room for God.

But although it is scientists *making* these statements, these are not *scientific statements*. They're not based on science—otherwise no scientists would be Christians. They're based on something else.

Stephen Hawking and Taylor Swift

Let's imagine for a moment that the great physicist Stephen Hawking is still alive (he actually died in 2018)—and you, yes you, have a chance to meet him. Hawking is renowned across the world for his research on black holes, and he's coming to your town to talk about it.

Hawking delivers a short talk that completely blows your mind. He talks about time, space, and the history of the universe. Wormholes, black holes, time travel, quantum mechanics—he touches on it all.

But then Hawking starts talking about the music of Taylor Swift. It becomes clear that he's only ever listened to two of her songs, but that doesn't stop him from delivering a whole bunch of opinions about each of her albums.

Stephen Hawking
1942–2018

Which topic are you most likely to trust Stephen Hawking on—black holes or Taylor Swift?

Obviously, black holes. That's what he's spent his life researching. He knows more about black holes than most people know about *anything*. Whereas he has no expertise at all in Taylor Swift songs.*

You can see that there's a difference between *statements made by scientists* and *statements based on science*. A scientist can have all sorts of opinions about all sorts of things—and we'd be right to listen to them as much as we listen to anybody else. (It's only polite.) But we don't need to assume that everything a

* I don't think Stephen Hawking would ever actually have given a lecture on Taylor Swift. But he did give his opinion on God. His friend Martin Rees, another important astrophysicist, didn't think Hawking was right to do so. He said, "I know Stephen Hawking well enough to know that he has read little philosophy and less theology, so I don't think his views [on God] should be taken with any special weight" (*The Guardian*, Wednesday 6th April 2011).

scientist says is definitely the truth simply because he or she is a scientist.

When one scientist says they find that science and faith in God work beautifully together, and another scientist says that they think science and faith in God are incompatible, we can assume that it isn't actually the science that is making them disagree. It's something else.

To understand what that something else is, we need to delve a bit further into this relationship between science and faith. We need to ask: what is science *for*?

In Short

- People often give Galileo as an example of the conflict between science and religion—but Galileo was a Christian, and his story is more complicated than it sometimes seems.
- Many scientists have a religious faith—60% of Nobel Prize winners between 1901 and 2000 were Christians. It's perfectly possible to believe in both science and God.
- When we hear some scientists say that you can't believe in both science and God, we should remember that not everything a scientist says is actually based on science.

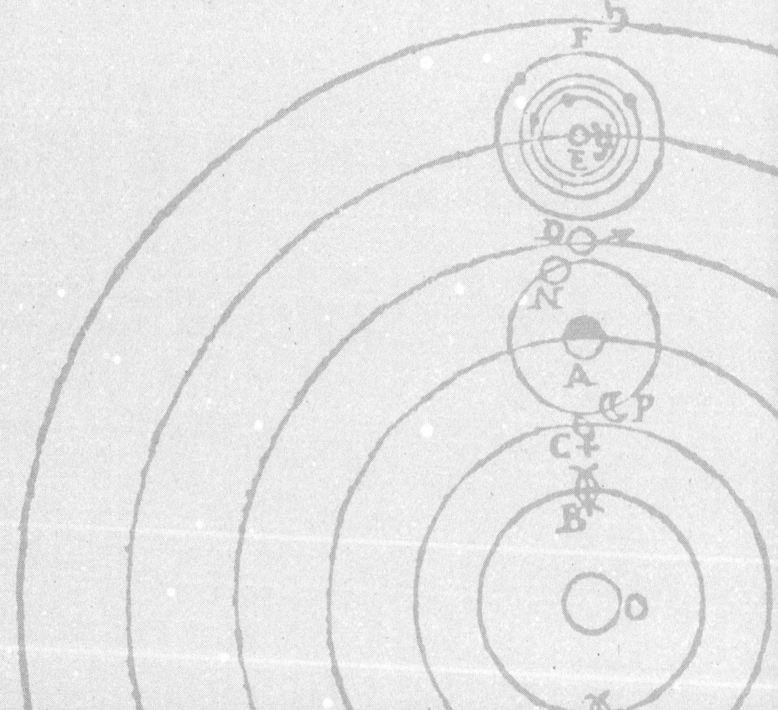

Chapter 2

BAKING A CAKE WITH AUNT MATILDA

What is science for?

Imagine that my Aunt Matilda has baked a cake. It's a Victoria sponge: two layers of vanilla-flavoured cake, with strawberry jam and cream in between, and a light dusting of icing sugar on top. Aunt Matilda has bought some fresh strawberries, too, and arranged them around the edge. It looks delicious.

Now imagine that you and I and Aunt Matilda decide to snatch this cake away from the hungry eyes of my family. Instead of eating it, we take it to a group of top scientists. "Please analyse this cake," we tell them. And they get to work.

The following day, the scientists submit their results. The biochemist goes first: she informs us about the proteins, fats and so on that are found in the cake. She has calculated how many calories each slice contains, and can tell us about how eating this cake will affect our bodies. Aunt Matilda asks whether it makes a difference if she eats a strawberry as well.

Second comes a chemist. He presents a list of all the chemical elements that can be found in the cake. He explains that while Aunt Matilda was mixing the batter, the baking soda (which he calls sodium bicarbonate) began to react with the milk. This created tiny bubbles of carbon dioxide, which then expanded in the heat of the oven—which is what caused the cake to rise.

We all nod interestedly, but before we have time to hear more, the physicist is taking over.

The physicist tells us about the cake on an even smaller level. She has calculated how many atoms there are in this cake, and begins to write the number on the blackboard in the corner of the lab. But before she can finish her extremely long number, she is shouldered aside by a mathematician, who takes a fresh piece of chalk and covers the board with a set of elegant equations. These describe and predict the behaviour of the particles in the cake.

But you are shaking your head. "I've learned a lot," you say, "but there's still one thing I don't understand. I know *how* the cake was made. I know *what* it was made of. But you haven't explained *why* it was made."

Aunt Matilda grins: *she* knows the answer. But the

scientists look dismayed. "We don't know *why*," they say. "That isn't what science is for!"

Can Science Explain Everything?

Lots of people today will tell you that belief in God is just not necessary. After all, science can explain so many things! The argument goes that in past centuries, nobody really understood how the universe worked, so they had to make things up—things like God—in order to find explanations for their experiences. Now that we know more, it would be silly to believe in God. We just don't need him!

I wonder if you've heard people say that. You may even have thought it yourself.

You may also have heard someone say that you have to choose between God and science. Either God is your explanation for everything, or science is. You can't have both.

This is the position of some of the scientists I mentioned in the previous chapter. They sign up to something called scientism. That means saying things like this:

> *Science is the* ***only way*** *to find out the truth about* ***anything****.*

That belief is the big difference between people who say that science and faith in God work together and people who say that they are incompatible. It isn't that the second group of people have found some scientific evidence that is being ignored by the first group of people. It's that they have a different basic belief.

One group thinks that science is the only way to find out the truth about anything. The other thinks that although science is important, there are other ways to find out other types of truth as well.

People who believe in scientism are usually very excited about all the things that science can do—and they're right to be! But they've lost sight of *what science is actually for.*

Science is really good at answering questions like "How does breathing work?" and "What is going on inside a black hole?" and "What makes rain happen?" It tells us about how the physical world works. But it doesn't deal with other big and important questions. Sir Peter Medawar, a Nobel Prize winner for biology, called them "childlike elementary questions": How did everything begin? What are we all here for? What is the point of living? He pointed out that science is limited because it can't answer those bigger questions that we all ask.*

(This is why you don't *only* study science at school, by the way. There's something important and meaningful about language, history, art, music and all the other subjects, right? They make you think about things that science will never help you with.)

The point is that science does not compete with God as an explanation of the world. They're just different kinds of explanation, focusing on different kinds of questions. That means you *don't* have to choose between science and God. It's perfectly possible to believe in both.

---

* He said this in his book *The Limits of Science* (OUP, 1984).

How Science Works

Time for a bit more detail.

Back before the Victorian times, what we now call "science" was known as "natural philosophy". Philosophy is essentially about *thinking*—so natural philosophy, or science, is a way of *thinking about the natural world.* It means figuring out how the world works. Sometimes that's at a very tiny level: cells, atoms and subatomic particles. Sometimes it's at a huge, universe-wide level: planets, stars and galaxies.

For example, did you know that if you stacked all the bacteria in the world on top of each other, they would stretch for 10 billion light years? That means they could wrap around the Milky Way galaxy over 20,000 times.

Or did you know that protons, one of the tiniest particles that exist, come in a range of shapes? Some are shaped like a peanut. Some are a sphere. Some look like a rugby ball. Some look like bagels!*

But *how* do scientists figure out things like this? The process they use is called "induction" or "inductive reasoning". Essentially what they do is this:

* Both these facts come from www.sciencefocus.com/science/fun-facts (accessed 13th February, 2024).

1. They make observations.

2. They look for possible explanations.

3. They test those explanations with experiments.

(By the way, this means that nothing in science is ever *completely* "proved". Scientists are simply looking for the best possible explanation to fit the facts. They often have enough evidence to make them very sure about their theories—but it's always possible that new information will turn up and they'll have to think again. We're going to talk more about this in the next chapter.)

Here's an example. For many hundreds of years, everyone assumed that if you dropped a heavy object and a light object from the same place at the same time, the heavier object would hit the ground first. It just made sense as a theory. Heavy things ought to fall faster than light things, right?

But in the 16th century, the Italian scientist Galileo (our old friend) decided to test that theory. The story goes that he took two balls that were the same size but different weights. He carried them all the way to the top of the Leaning Tower of Pisa. He dropped them. And they hit the ground at the *same time*. The heavier one did *not* fall faster than the lighter one.

Galileo was a scientist. He was doing an experiment that tested a theory. His observations led to a whole new understanding of how gravity works. And that changed the way scientists understood all kinds of things—including space, planets and how to send a rocket to the moon.

In other words, science is both extremely impressive and very useful!

The Laws of Nature

But as we've seen already, science has limits.

Since we've been talking about gravity, let's ask: what does the law of gravity explain?

You probably know something about gravity already. Here's a quick summary:*

- Gravity is a force that exists everywhere.
- It pulls all things with mass or energy toward one another.
- We commonly experience gravity by being pulled downwards by the earth.
- Gravity keeps all of the planets in orbit around the sun. It also keeps the moon in orbit around the earth.

---

* This comes from the BBC Bitesize website.

Now here's a more complicated version:

> *The law of gravity states that every particle attracts every other particle in the universe with a force that is proportional to the product of their masses...*

In other words, the heavier an object is, the more it pulls other objects towards it (which is why we are all pulled towards the earth).

> *... and inversely proportional to the square of the distance between their centres.*

In other words, the closer two objects are, the more they are pulled towards each other (which is why we don't all get dragged away from the earth, which is close, towards the sun, which is bigger but further away).

This law was put together by Isaac Newton, an English scientist who was working about a hundred years after Galileo.

So that's gravity. Now back to our question: what does Newton's law of gravitation explain?

It explains gravity, yes?

Well, does it?

Newton's law enables us to know *what happens because of* gravity. It has allowed us to work out the paths that the planets take around the sun, for example. But it doesn't explain what gravity itself actually *is*—not really. Nor does it explain *why* it exists.

Of course, more science may give us more understanding. In fact, it already has. Albert Einstein's theory of General Relativity states that gravity is a curving of space-time. But this remains very hard to grasp, and there are still big gaps in physicists' knowledge.

Even if we do figure out a satisfactory explanation of what gravity is, though, we will still have questions—because science has limits. We already know that science can't answer important questions about what life is all about. But it also can't answer questions like: Why does gravity exist? Why does it always work in a predictable way? Why is the universe ordered and understandable at all?

Science tells us how the world works, but it can't tell us *why* it exists in the way it does.

We need science to understand the world—that's definitely true. But science isn't all we need.

In Short

- Scientism is the belief that science is the only way to find out the truth about anything. This belief is what leads some people to say you have to choose between God and science.
- Although science is very good at answering questions about how the physical world works, there are other questions it can't answer—such as questions about how we should live and what life is all about.
- Science can make observations and enable us to make predictions, but it can't explain why the universe exists or why it is the way it is.
- In other words, there are types of truth that science can't get at. We need science, but science isn't all we need to find out the truth about the world.

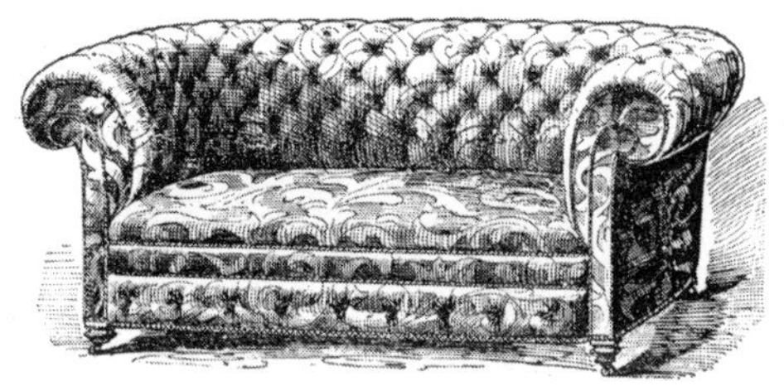

Chapter 3

DO YOU TRUST YOUR SOFA?

Why you can't do science without faith

Hopefully you agree by now that science and faith in God *can* exist alongside each other. They're answering different sorts of questions, so they're not really in conflict. But you might still be wondering whether they *need* to exist alongside each other. What if you just don't particularly want to believe in God? Plenty of people live their lives without believing in him, don't they?

One response is to say that, of course, it's true that many people *don't* believe in God. But in my experience, many of them have not really considered the evidence for God. They've just decided he doesn't exist. That's not very scientific!

Another answer is to say that in fact, *nobody* lives their life without faith! Not only that but... and this might surprise you... *you can't do science without faith.*

Let me explain.

You Gotta Have Faith

When we say the word "faith", we often mean religious faith, but actually the word "faith" just means "trust" or "belief". And that's something we all need—and use—every day.

For instance, you have faith in the chair or sofa or bed you're sitting on right now: you're trusting it not to collapse under you. You have faith in your bus driver: you trust that he or she can drive the bus safely and won't crash. You have faith in the people who work in the cafeteria at school: you believe that they're not trying to poison you.

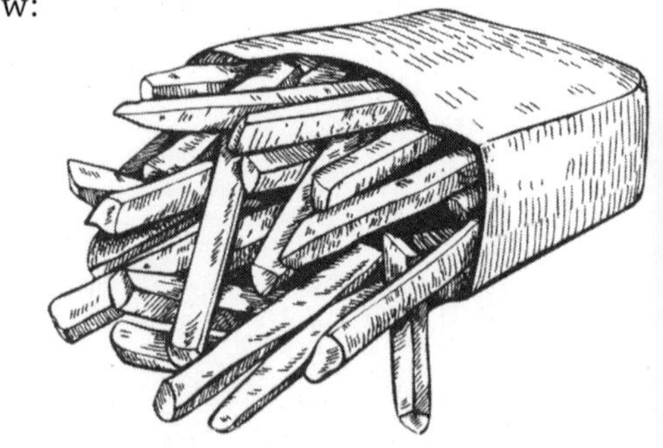

Imagine what life would be like if you didn't have faith! You'd never be able to do *anything*.

Sometimes people talk as if faith means putting your trust in something you have absolutely no evidence for. But that's *blind* faith. Most of the time, faith isn't blind.

Most of the time, faith means putting your trust in something that you do have evidence for.

To go back to the school cafeteria, do you know for certain that the food there is safe to eat? No, you don't! It's possible that the cooks *are* trying to poison you. You don't have 100% rock-solid certainty that they aren't. But you do have good *evidence*. Given that they haven't poisoned you on Monday, Tuesday, Wednesday or Thursday, it stands to reason that they won't make the attempt on Friday either. Your faith in those cooks is quite sensible.

This is the type of faith that scientists use too. We saw in the last chapter that scientists are always looking for the best possible explanation to fit their observations. Technically, they don't have 100% *proof* about their conclusions. They do have evidence—often really good evidence. They've repeated their experiments and got the same results again and again, just like you eating the school cooks' food every day and not getting ill. But there is always the possibility that the result will change next time, or that when other information is added, things will look different. Scientists still need to believe in the conclusions they've reached, just like you still need to believe in your school cooks.

Just like all of us, scientists need faith.

Faith That Science Works

In fact, the great physicist Albert Einstein once said that he couldn't imagine a genuine scientist who didn't have "profound faith".* What faith was he speaking of? Not faith in God (although Einstein did believe that there is some sort of God). What Einstein meant was faith that the world can be understood using science and reason: that is, faith that science *works*.

"Of course science works," I hear you say—but when you really think about it, it's quite surprising and amazing that science works.

Imagine you're a physicist sitting at a desk somewhere, looking at some equations. You're just a little blob of humanity, one person among billions, on a small planet that occupies a tiny fragment of the universe. And yet the equations that you're working on can describe the movement of planets and the age of stars. There are mathematical symbols on the paper in front of you, written down using an old biro and a bit of ancient Greek, which express something true about the universe—a universe that is so vast, you can't even fully imagine it.

Isn't that *incredible?*

A physicist called Eugene Wigner famously wrote that mathematics is "unreasonably effective".** He pointed out that the theory of gravity was originally based on just a few, rather imperfect observations of what happens to rocks when you throw them. It is incredibly surprising, then, that this same theory can accurately describe much grander things like the movement of

* "Science and Religion", in *Nature* No. 3706 (9th November, 1940). You can read it here: www.nature.com/articles/146605a0.pdf (accessed 23rd October 2018).

** "The Unreasonable Effectiveness of Mathematics in the Natural Sciences", in *Communications in Pure and Applied Mathematics,* Vol. 13, No. 1 (February 1960). You can read it here: www.maths.ed.ac.uk/~v1ranick/papers/wigner.pdf (accessed 6th August 2024).

planets. Using Newton's law to understand space seems rather like building a supercomputer out of Duplo. But amazingly, it works!

This led Wigner to an unsettling thought. The theories that scientists rely on are amazingly effective at explaining many of the things that they observe. But *so are theories that we know to be false.* For example, J.J. Thomson discovered electrons in 1897. He theorised that atoms were like "plum puddings": balls of positively charged matter, studded with electrons. Thomson's theory is good enough to explain a lot about magnets and electricity—the theory works! But it was later found to be *wrong*. Scientists now understand that the atom is much more complex than that.

Wigner worried, what if our current theories are just like Thomson's plum-pudding idea? Isn't it quite likely that one day we'll discover that even though our theories were very effective, they were not quite right after all?

Scientists have a lot of evidence to back up their conclusions. But they still need to decide to trust that evidence and believe in those conclusions.

Are you starting to see how much faith you need in order to do science?

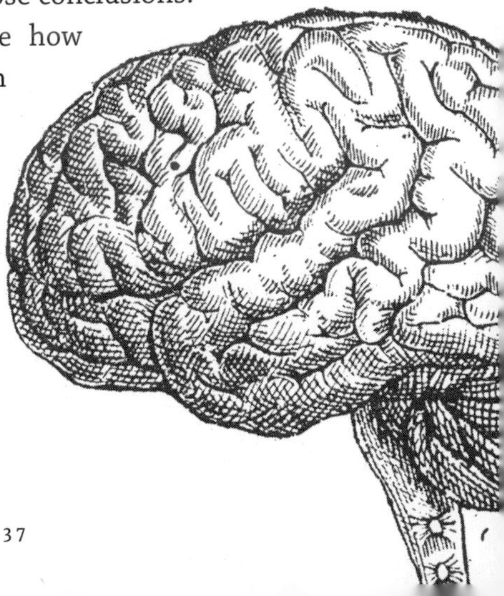

Can You Trust Your Brain?

It's not just physics that requires faith. There are issues much closer to home as well.

Here's a conversation I've had many times with fellow scientists:

"What do you do science with?" I ask.

"My brain," they respond.

"Tell me about your brain," I request. "How did it come to exist?"

If the person I am talking to is an atheist, they say something like "It came to exist by means of natural, mindless, unguided processes." Or they might say that it happened by chance and the laws of nature—according to the theory of evolution.

Then I ask, "If you thought that your computer was the result of mindless, unguided processes, would you trust it?"

"Not in a million years!" comes the reply. A computer only works because it has been designed by intelligent humans.

"Well, then," I say, "why do you trust your brain?"

Do you see the problem?

Here's another example. Imagine your biology teacher hands you a textbook. "This was put together randomly," she says, "by a monkey typing on a typewriter." What would you think? Would you trust that textbook? Of course not—that monkey doesn't know anything about biology, nor can

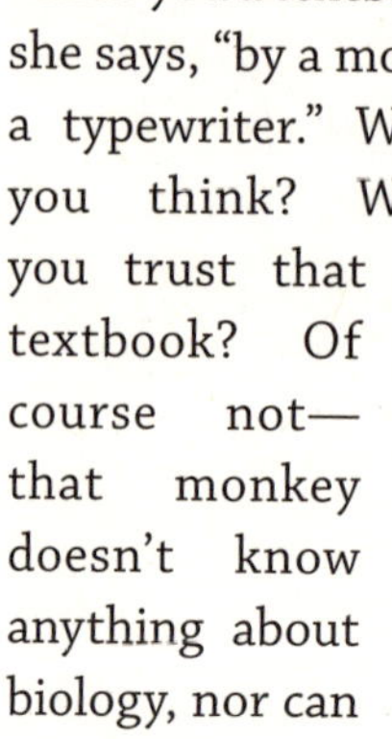

it speak English. A textbook typed out at random isn't a textbook; it's just gibberish. So is anything that arises from pure chance.

So if our brains evolved through mindless, unguided processes, why should we trust them?*

Yet we all put our faith in our brains every single day.

A Deeper Cause

The orderedness of the universe, along with the fact that human brains can understand it, are things of great wonder. It isn't just obvious that they are true—it's actually very surprising. As Einstein and others have recognised, we need to have a lot of faith in our brains and in the orderedness of the universe in order to even start doing science.

And this brings us back to God, because many scientists, having observed the amazing truth that science works, decide that God is the best explanation.

The mathematics professor Hannah Fry and the biologist Adam Rutherford (neither of whom believe in God) once recorded a podcast in which they discussed a certain number which has many surprising uses in maths.** Here's part of their conversation:

---

* Charles Darwin himself (the person who first came up with the theory of evolution) also acknowledged this problem. He believed that humans are descended from apes—but he wrote about a "horrid doubt" that regularly came into his mind: "Would anyone trust in the convictions of a monkey's mind, if there are any convictions in such a mind?" (*Letter to William Graham*, 3rd July 1881). You can read the whole letter at: goo.gl/Jfyu9Q (accessed 28th June 2018).

** The number is pi (or π, or 3.1415926-ish). You might know that pi is used for working out the circumference of a circle, but there are a lot of other calculations it appears in too.

Adam (the biologist): You get a little bit, sort of, almost mystical about the universality – you know, the way it pops up in all these weird places that you didn't expect. When YOU get mystical, I'm like, oh, this is interesting.

Hannah (the mathematician): The thing is… I've tried to explain this before, and it's just not something that you can really use words to describe. It's something that you can only know about if you have tried to understand the universe using mathematics. Because you are left in absolutely no doubt that you are on this voyage of… of a path that is not human-made. I mean, I can't describe it in any better way.

Adam: That is truly fascinating, because we know that of all the sciences, mathematics – if you're counting it as a science – is the one that has the highest proportion of religious people in it.

These two scientists do not believe in God. But they acknowledge that for many people, the amazing orderedness of the universe and the amazing effectiveness of science in describing it are two huge reasons to believe in God.

Here's how the philosopher Richard Swinburne puts it:*

* In his book *Is There a God?* (OUP, 1996), page 68.

> The very success of science in showing us how deeply orderly the natural world is provides strong grounds for believing that there is an even deeper cause for that order.

When Swinburne and others like him look at the world and consider what we know about it, it just seems to make sense to believe that someone *designed* the universe and the human brain.

We're starting to see that believing in God and believing in science aren't just compatible. Believing in God may actually make science make *more* sense than it does without him.

The Faith of Atheists

There's one more thing to say about faith before we finish this chapter.

You will have realised by now that *not* believing in God is just as much a matter of faith as believing in him is. Do atheists have proof that God doesn't exist, that the universe came about by chance, and that science is the only way to find out the truth about anything? No, they don't. They may believe that that is where the evidence leads—but *belief* means faith.

I once found myself in a conversation about this with a world-famous atheist called Peter Singer. We were in Melbourne, Australia, and we were holding a big public debate about the existence of God. To introduce myself, I told the audience that I grew up in Northern Ireland and that my parents were Christians.

Peter Singer immediately seized on this. "This is one of my objections to religion," he said. He explained that people often carry on with the religious faith their parents had. It's just a matter of upbringing, he claimed, not about what's really true.

"Peter," I responded, "can I ask you—were your parents atheists?"

"Yes," he replied, "my mother was."

"So," I said to Peter, "you're carrying on your parent's faith too, then, just like me."

He was taken aback. "It's not faith!" he cried.

"But I thought you believed it," I answered.

It was all over the internet afterwards. How could it be that this famous philosopher did not realise that atheism is a belief system—that *not* believing in God involves faith, just like believing in him does? Peter rejected God as an explanation of why the universe is the way it is, and he put his faith in other ideas instead. But he was still a person of faith.

And so are you. The question is, what are you putting your faith in—and why?

In Short

- Faith works together with evidence to make us sure about something. We all put our faith in things every day.
- Scientists need faith in order to do science. They need faith that science will work.
- It's really amazing and surprising that science works—that the universe is ordered and consistent, and that we can understand it using our brains.
- So, many scientists say that it's actually easier to trust in science if you trust in a God who designed the world.
- People who don't believe in God are still people of faith.

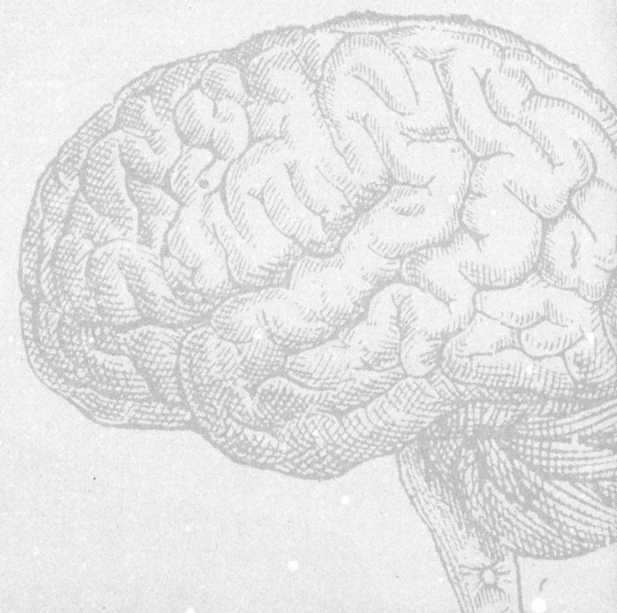

Chapter 4

ZEUS'S THUNDERBOLTS AND THE GOD OF THE GAPS

Is it reasonable to believe in God?

Have you ever wondered how life on Earth began?

In the 1920s, two scientists came up with more or less the same answer to that question. One was the Russian biochemist Aleksandr Oparin, and the other was a British scientist called J.B.S. Haldane. They suggested that millions of years ago, there was a lot of methane, ammonia, hydrogen and water vapour, plus a few other ingredients, all bubbling away in a "primordial soup". Nothing in this soup was alive. But then, all of a sudden (they theorised), some compounds called amino acids were formed—possibly because of a lightning strike which kick-started certain chemical reactions.

Amino acids can combine together to make up proteins, and proteins are what you need for cells, and cells are what living things are made of. So, amino acids are often described as the basic building blocks of life. From a primordial soup to the beginnings of life! That's how Oparin and Haldane thought it must have happened. And that's how many people still assume it happened.

Yet there are problems with this theory.

Uncertainty

Most geochemists now think differently about which compounds were around at the relevant point in the earth's history. It now seems to them that the atmosphere of the early earth would actually have *prevented* amino acids from forming. But there's an even more serious difficulty than that. In one of the biggest discoveries of the 20th century, it was found that amino acids can't become the building blocks of life until they are connected together in a particular order in very long chains.

Why is this a problem for the "primordial soup" hypothesis? Because it's extremely unlikely that this could happen by chance.

And I mean *extremely* unlikely. It's been said that the likelihood of life starting from non-life, just like that, is about the same as the likelihood of a tornado ripping through a junkyard and accidentally assembling a Boeing 747 aircraft.* It might just be possible in theory, but it's so improbable, it would never *actually* happen.

Other theories have also been put forward. But the honest answer to the question, "How did life on Earth begin?" is that scientists aren't sure.

Now you might expect me to say, "Therefore, God *must* have started life on Earth! It's the only possible explanation. We *must* have a Creator!"

But making that kind of argument would be a mistake.

As a matter of fact, I do believe that God is the one who got life started on our planet. But I don't believe it *just* because scientists haven't come up with a definite explanation.

God of the Gaps

I want you to imagine for a moment that you have grown up believing in Zeus—the Greek god of lightning.

Every time there is a storm, you look out of your window and shudder at the rumbling thunder and flashes of light. You know that what you're seeing is Zeus hurling a thunderbolt through the sky, and you fear for those who are feeling the full effects of his anger.

Now imagine that you go to school one day, and your physics teacher announces that the topic for today's lesson is lightning.

You listen in amazement as you discover how electrical charges build up inside clouds as ice crystals rub

* The mathematician Sir Fred Hoyle was the person who first made this comparison.

together. The lecturer explains that a flash of lightning is a huge spark that discharges this built-up electricity. In other words, lightning and thunder are just a giant version of the snap that happens when you've rubbed a balloon against your woolly sweater and then someone touches you.

You stare at your teacher as the penny finally drops: *Zeus isn't real.*

You believed in Zeus because you needed an explanation for thunder and lightning. But now you have a better explanation—one based on science. So you don't need Zeus anymore. It makes no sense to believe in him, now that you know what you know.

This is because Zeus is what we call a "god of the gaps".

Throughout history, many people have believed in various gods because they wanted explanations for things they had no other way of understanding. The gods filled the gaps in people's knowledge. But as science has developed, many of those gaps have gone away. We don't need to believe in a god of lightning anymore because lightning isn't a gap anymore: we know how it works.

So if your *only* reason to believe in God is "We don't know how life on Earth began; therefore there must be a God who miraculously made it happen," you're making the same error as the ancient Greeks. You're believing in yet another god of the gaps—it's just a different gap. If scientists discover more about what was going on in the very earliest stages of the earth, the gap might go away, and so will your belief in God.

By contrast, the reason why *I* think God is the person who started off life on Earth is that I have lots of other reasons to believe that he exists and that he created the world. My belief in God doesn't depend on a particular gap, or even on a combination of gaps. There's other evidence that has persuaded me of God's existence.

We'll get to the most important evidence for believing in God in chapter 7. By then we'll be focusing on Christian beliefs specifically. But first, let's look at evidence that *some sort of Creator* exists, without zeroing in on a particular religion.

The God Hypothesis

Let's say you've decided to make a roast dinner, and you're looking at a recipe. Perhaps it begins like this:

- *Preheat oven to 180C / 350F.*
- *Roughly chop 1 onion and 2 carrots.*
- *Scatter onion and carrots across the base of a roasting tin.*
- *Sit 1 whole chicken on top of the vegetables.*

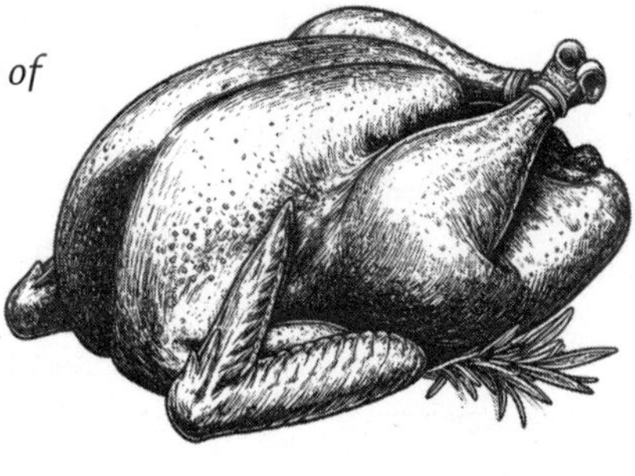

The question is, how did those words come about?

Your answer is probably that a chef wrote them. And that's very reasonable. Language comes from people. (Even if the words come via AI, that AI still needs to have been given information by a human.) Faced with words, it's reasonable to assume that a human mind is behind them.

This is not a "mind of the gaps" argument. You're not saying, "There is no explanation; therefore it must have been a person." Instead, you are thinking through the evidence—which includes all the experience of writing and language you've had in your life—and you're putting forward the explanation that fits best with that evidence: a human being designed this recipe and wrote these words.

Antony Flew
1923–2010

In the same way, plenty of people have looked at the world and decided that the best explanation for the way it works is that it has a Creator or designer. In other words, they put forward the God hypothesis.*

One such person was the philosophy professor Antony Flew.

The Language of DNA

It was quite big news when, in 2004, Professor Flew decided that he believed in an intelligent Creator. He had been a well-known atheist for most of his life. He had even written books arguing for atheism and had persuaded lots of other people to be atheists too! But

* A hypothesis just means a scientist's best guess. It means, "I'm not completely sure, but taking all the evidence into account, I think it *probably* happened this way."

now he decided that there must be some sort of God. He explained:*

> My whole life has been guided by the principle … "Follow the evidence wherever it leads."

What changed Flew's mind was some new evidence that biologists had discovered about DNA.

DNA is a bit like the words in your roast chicken recipe. It's a set of instructions—a code that tells the cells in your body what to do.

The thing is, your recipe wouldn't be at all useful if it read like this:

Oe9Csgrb vhe01ar/ gHweruxw
s2h phCn wegh wxcWeloij wro.rughawe
thwEE wefoijwejc, pobcxzLKJ vn.7

Instructions are only instructions if they have actual words in them, and words are only words if the letters are in the right order. In just the same way, DNA only works if the "letters" inside it come in the right order. (The "letters" are molecules called nucleotides, which have to be connected in specific ways in order to work.)

When Flew understood this, he decided that the best explanation for the existence of DNA was some

* Antony Flew, *There Is a God* (Harper Collins, 2007), page 123.

sort of intelligent designer. Just as you see a recipe and realise that a mind must be behind it, so Flew saw the way DNA works and decided that a mind must be behind that too.

This is different from believing in Zeus, because it involves actually looking at evidence. Flew saw the observations that scientists had made and formed the conclusion, based on evidence, that an intelligent mind was responsible for life on our planet.

A Finely Tuned Universe

There are also discoveries of more cosmic proportions that persuade some scientists to believe that God exists.

We are gradually discovering that the fundamental forces in the universe are amazingly delicately balanced, or "fine-tuned", to support life. Many different aspects of the universe—from the energy levels in carbon atoms to the rate at which the universe is expanding—turn out to be exactly what they need to be for life to be possible. Change any of them just a little, and we would not exist.

For example, life wouldn't exist without stars. To be more precise, we need *both* large stars, which are like huge machines that produce crucial elements like oxygen and carbon, *and* small stars (like our sun), which burn long enough to provide the long-term warmth that is required for life. The theoretical physicist Paul Davies tells us that, happily, the forces of gravity and electromagnetism are delicately balanced in such a way that the universe includes both large stars and small stars. But if you changed the strength of one of those forces just slightly, you'd have big problems.

What do I mean by "just slightly"? Davies explains that the accuracy that is needed is the same level of accuracy that you would need to shoot a gun and hit a coin at the far side of the universe—that's 20 billion light years away. It's *very* unlikely that anyone would make that shot successfully. But that is how accurately balanced the forces of gravity and electromagnetism have to be in order for life to exist.

Davies concludes:*

> The impression of design is overwhelming.

The God of the Whole Show

I hope you're getting the point that believing in God can be rational—it's a reasonable way of understanding the evidence that science shows us.

But it doesn't make sense to believe in any old god. It doesn't make sense to believe in a god who exists *within* the universe, like Zeus or Thor, and serves as an explanation for particular things we observe in the world. No, we have to be talking about a Creator God: someone who designed the universe and set the whole thing in motion. Someone who exists beyond the world we know. This is the only kind of God science can point us towards.

But our problem now is that scientific findings can only go so far. Biology, physics and chemistry might

* *The Cosmic Blueprint* (Simon and Schuster, 1988), page 203.

suggest that there is indeed a Creator of this wondrous universe. But they can't give us much certainty about what that Creator could be like.

However, many religious believers say that there definitely *is* a God, and that you can get to know him!

What we need to do next, then, is examine that claim as carefully—and scientifically—as we can.

In Short

- We should avoid "God of the gaps" thinking—which means saying, "We don't know how something happened, so it must have been caused by God."
- However, this doesn't mean it's unreasonable to believe in God. Science leaves that open as a possible explanation for the world.
- DNA works in a similar way to language, and language can only come about from intelligent minds—so some people think that DNA is evidence that there is an intelligent designer for the world.
- Another argument for a Creator comes from physicists' observations about how finely tuned the universe is.

Chapter 5

MOUNTAIN GOATS AND METAPHORS

Is the Bible scientific?

According to Christianity, the best way to find out about God is to consider Jesus. He is God himself, who was born as a human, grew up at a particular time and in a particular place, and died. (And rose again, but we'll talk about that later.) We can find things out about Jesus because he isn't out there mysteriously in space—he lived a normal human life in history. (Well, normal-ish.) And knowing about Jesus means we can know about God.

There are four different accounts of Jesus' life in the Bible. One of them, written by a man named Luke, tells us why he wrote it:

> *Since I myself have carefully investigated everything from the beginning, I too decided to write an orderly account for you ... so that you may know the certainty of the things you have been taught. (Luke 1:3-4)*

Luke had gathered the evidence about Jesus, and now he was inviting readers to consider it. That sounds encouragingly like the same rational process that we use in science. History is not the same as the natural sciences, but it is still based on reasoning. Later in this book, we're going to consider some of the evidence Luke and others put forward to support their claims about Jesus.

But before we do that, we need to pause and clear some ground. All the evidence I've just mentioned comes from the Bible, the Christian holy book. So we need to start by thinking about whether this book can be trusted by scientists in the first place.

Hopefully you're convinced by now that science and God aren't enemies. But some would say that science and the Bible *are* enemies. So we need to ask whether that's true.

What the Bible Talks About

Here's something that's important to understand up front: although the Bible does take evidence seriously, it is *not* a science textbook and shouldn't be treated like one.

This is something that has tripped a lot of people up, and I don't want it to do the same to you!

If the Bible were a science textbook, it would focus on making lots of statements about the natural world and how it works. Whereas in fact, it is mostly interested in what life is all about, what God is like, and how to live well—very different questions altogether.

That's not to say that the Bible doesn't say anything true about the natural world, however.

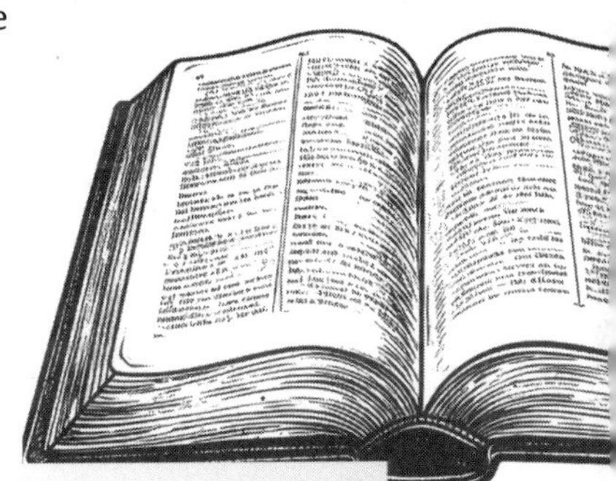

For example, the very first sentence of the Bible tells us that the universe had a beginning:

> *In the beginning God created the heavens and the earth. (Genesis 1:1)*

These days, the idea that the universe had a beginning is not very controversial. We all know that that beginning is called the Big Bang. (Though of course we don't all agree about whether God is the person who started that beginning off.) But did you know that scientists only came up with this idea about a hundred years ago?

For centuries, most people thought that the universe was eternal—it had always been more or less the same, existing in what was called a "steady state". Even Albert Einstein thought this! But in the 1920s, astronomers started to realise that the universe was expanding. And if something is getting bigger and bigger, that means it must have once been smaller and smaller. In 1931, a Belgian cosmologist called Georges Lemaître proposed that the universe has *always* been getting bigger—and that therefore the universe must have had a beginning. Once upon a time, there was nothing but a single "atom". And then, for some reason, the great expansion began.

At first, many scientists did not like this idea one bit! In fact, the "Big Bang" name was originally designed to poke fun at it. How stupid to believe that a "big bang" started the universe! People accused Georges Lemaître of being desperate to believe that the universe had a beginning—after all, he was a priest as well as a cosmologist. They were suspicious of how conveniently the Big Bang theory fitted with Lemaître's belief in the Bible.

But gradually, the evidence mounted, and nowadays pretty much *everyone* thinks that the universe had a beginning. Which is indeed exactly what the Bible has been saying all along.

So, the Bible does contain statements about the natural world, and Christians take those statements seriously. But most of the time, the Bible doesn't answer the questions that scientists are asking—about things like how old the stars are, or what elements are involved in the formation of planets, or how gravity works. Remember, Christianity is much more about "what's life all about" questions than it is about "how does the physical universe work" questions.

Ignorance and Awe

In fact, the Bible's human writers were deeply aware of how little they knew about scientific questions. A good example of this is in the book of Job. There's a whole chapter in this book where God challenges Job, the main character, because he doesn't know very much science! God asks lots of questions which expose Job's ignorance. These include questions about space:

> *Do you know the laws of the heavens?*
> *Can you set up God's dominion over the earth?*
> *(Job 38:33)*

And questions about the weather:

> *What is the way to the place where the lightning is dispersed,*
> *or the place where the east winds are scattered over the earth? (38:24)*

And questions about animal behaviour:

> *Do you know when the mountain goats give birth?*
> *Do you watch when the doe bears her fawn?*
> *(39:1)*

And lots of other questions too!

The answer to all these questions is "Errr, no, I don't know." So the point this passage is making is that *there's a lot we humans don't know.*

In other words, the Bible definitely doesn't claim to have all the answers to how the world works. Often, it just invites us to just sit back and say, "Wow!"

The Ostrich Laughs

This passage in the book of Job tells us something else about the way the Bible talks about the natural world, too. It uses metaphors. That means it sometimes talks about one thing as if it's another thing.

For example: Jesus once said, "I am the door" (John 10:9). Did Jesus literally mean that he was a door? No! We all know what doors are like: flattish, hinged, and made of wood or other hard materials. Jesus was not any of those things. He is not a literal door. But that's not to say that Jesus' statement was meaningless. He simply meant that he is the doorway to God—it's through him that we can have a relationship with God. Jesus was using a metaphor that stood for a reality.

The passage in Job uses metaphorical language too. It talks about the sea being shut up behind doors and bursting forth from a womb (38:8). It says that the clouds are clothes (38:9) and the snow is kept in storehouses (38:22). It says that an ostrich "laughs" at a horse (39:18). None of this is meant to be *literally* true. It's just being poetic. It's using metaphors to help us imagine real seas, clouds, snow and animals in a vivid way.

My point is that "literal" and "true" are not exactly the same thing.

It is true that snow falls at some times and not others, but it is not literally stored up in storehouses during the summer. It is true that an ostrich can run much faster than a horse, but she doesn't literally laugh as she goes past. It is true (Christians claim) that Jesus is the door, but he is not literally a door.

Christians think that it is important to believe that the Bible is true. We should take what it says very seriously. But something can be true without being literal. And it's very important to remember that when we look at statements the Bible makes about the natural world.

A Fixed Earth?

Which brings us back to one of history's big bust-ups (so they say) between science and religion: Copernicus, Galileo, and the relationship between the sun and the earth.

Back in the 3rd century BC, the Greek philosopher Aristotle taught that the earth was fixed in the centre of the universe and that the sun, stars and planets revolved around it. That view remained the usual one for centuries. It made sense. After all, the sun rises and sets—it appears to go around the earth. And, if the earth moved, wouldn't we all be flung into space? Wouldn't things drop sideways instead of down?

This fixed-earth, moving-sun interpretation also seemed to fit in well with what the Bible says:

> *[God] set the earth on its foundations;*
> *it can never be moved. (Psalm 104:5)*

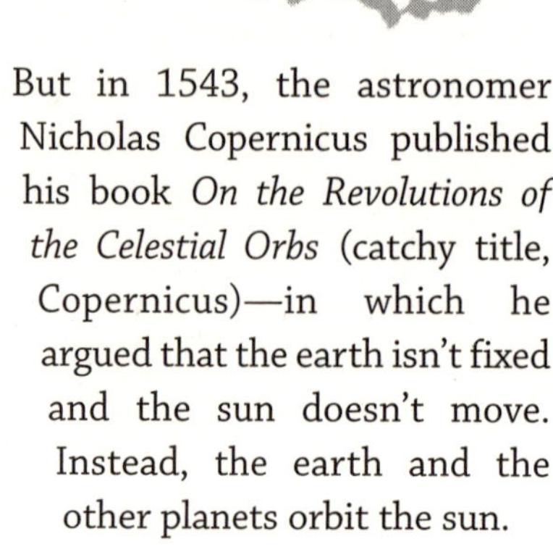

But in 1543, the astronomer Nicholas Copernicus published his book *On the Revolutions of the Celestial Orbs* (catchy title, Copernicus)—in which he argued that the earth isn't fixed and the sun doesn't move. Instead, the earth and the other planets orbit the sun.

Nicholas Copernicus
1473–1543

Important religious people objected. Then, when Galileo added his own evidence to Copernicus' view, they objected again. And we all know what happened next.

But *does* the Bible contradict the idea that the earth goes round the sun?

It does if you take verses like Psalm 104:5 (the one I just quoted) literally. But as we know, it's perfectly reasonable not to take those verses literally. It's more likely that Psalm 104:5 is saying something metaphorical. Psalm 104, a bit like the passage from Job, is inviting us to say, "Wow!" The message is something like: *This complicated world was made by someone extremely powerful and clever, and that same someone keeps it working the way it does. That's amazing!*

When we understand it properly, the Bible doesn't contradict today's scientific understanding of the relationship between the sun and the planets. But it does remind us to be wowed by it.

The Age of the Earth, and Other Questions

But this is not the only statement that the Bible makes about the natural world.

In this chapter we've mainly talked about the poetic parts of the Bible, where metaphors are used abundantly to describe the world and the things God has done. But there are also many parts of the Bible that aren't poetic, but historical—in other words, they make claims that certain things really happened.

In the first part of the Bible, the Old Testament, we're told lots of information about the history of the people of Israel—where they lived, who ruled them, how they interacted with other nations and so on. And in the second part, the New Testament, we're told lots of information about Jesus and the first men and women who followed him.

Some of those claims are obviously true. Archaeological evidence has been found for the existence of King David, a major figure in the Old Testament, for example. And all historians agree that Jesus was a real man who lived and died.

But what about when the Bible makes claims that seem to contradict other knowledge? In particular, what about those places where the Bible says something happened which seems to contradict science?

That's what we're going to look at in the next chapter.

In Short

- The Bible mainly focuses on "what's life all about" type questions rather than scientific ones—although it does make statements about the physical world.
- The Bible contains lots of metaphorical language. It's possible to believe that the Bible is true without taking everything it says literally.
- This means that although some have claimed that the Bible contradicts science in some of its statements about the natural world, these aren't actually conflicts at all.

Chapter 6

THE CHOCOLATE THIEF

Do ideas about miracles and creation contradict science?

Here's a test for you. Imagine someone told you that one of the following things has happened not far from where you live. Which would you be most likely to believe?

- Three people have gone inside a blazing fire and come out unhurt.
- A woman was able to fill every single bottle and pot in her village with the oil from just one small jar. She kept pouring it into other containers, and it didn't run out.

- Two men have walked across the surface of a lake (and it wasn't frozen over).
- A big jug of water has suddenly become wine, without anyone touching it.

What do you think? Perhaps your brain is running wild thinking of possible explanations. Maybe the people in the fire were wearing those silver suits that volcano scientists wear, which kept them safe? Maybe the woman actually had a secret pipe that led to a huge vat of oil? The men on the lake must have had some clever floating devices, some sort of shoes that kept them on the surface of the water—didn't Leonardo da Vinci invent something like that?*

* You can read about walking on water here: www.sciencefocus.com/nature/could-we-make-shoes-that-let-us-walk-on-water (accessed 7th April 2025).

Whether you came up with those ideas or not, I'm willing to bet that if someone told you that one of those things had happened in your home town, you wouldn't just believe them. At the very least, you'd ask some questions. Because you don't expect miracles like that to happen.

That's very reasonable. After all, we know that the world generally obeys the laws of nature (by which I mean the rules that science has observed about how the world works). Fire burns. Humans can't walk on water. And one thing doesn't just suddenly become another for no reason.

One of the best things about science is discovering explanations for things that might otherwise have seemed miraculous. You've probably seen chemistry experiments where you pour one liquid into another, and the mixture changes colour, or starts to smoke, or goes solid. That's not normally what happens when two liquids mix! So it seems like a miracle—until the person doing the experiment explains what's happened at a molecular level, and it all makes sense. Not a miracle after all.

But those four events I listed a moment ago are all examples of things that the Bible says are *real* miracles.* They really happened, and they happened for supernatural reasons.

According to some, we have a problem here. Aren't the laws of nature being broken? Is the Bible contradicting science?

---

* Here are the Bible passages in case you want to look them up: Daniel 3:19-27; 2 Kings 4:1-7; Matthew 14:25-29; John 2:1-10.

The Laws of Nature

It's pretty important that the laws of nature remain consistent. That's what enables us to do science at all. If you want to send something into space, you need gravity to keep on doing the same thing that it's always done. If you want to design a fast car, you need your steel and rubber to behave in the same way that steel and rubber have always behaved. If you want to breed giraffes, you need their reproductive cycles to follow the same timing they usually follow.

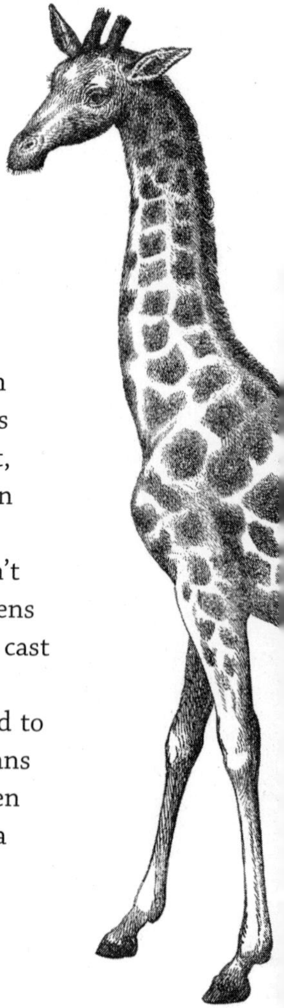

In all of those examples, scientists can make observations about the natural world (about gravity, steel, rubber and giraffes) and then use those observations to predict what will happen in the future. They couldn't do that if the laws of nature didn't remain the same. In fact, pretty much *everything* we do depends on the laws of nature being consistent.

You can see why some people really don't like the idea of miracles. If something happens that is normally impossible, doesn't that cast doubt on everything scientists do?

But this objection isn't actually that hard to answer. The crucial thing is that Christians don't believe in random miracles that happen with no explanation. They believe in a *person* who makes the miracles happen.

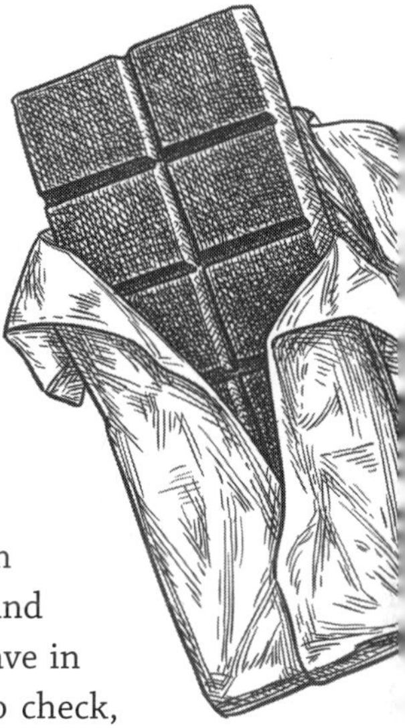

A Chocolatey Comparison

Imagine you have a large bar of chocolate. You don't want to eat it right now, but you also don't want your sister to get at it, so you hide it in your sock drawer. The following week, you add another bar of chocolate. The third week, you add another bar to your stash. Soon afterwards, you're at a friend's house, and he asks you how much chocolate you have in your sock drawer. You can't go home to check, but you don't need to: you know the answer. One plus one plus one is always three. So, you confidently tell your friend, "I've got three bars of chocolate."

But when you get home, you open your drawer and find that there's only one bar of chocolate in there!

What would you conclude?

Would you declare, "I can never trust maths again! One plus one plus one isn't three anymore!"?

Of course not. The laws of mathematics have not been broken—no, someone has intervened. What you would do is to march straight to your sister's room and demand to know what she has done with your chocolate!

Likewise, it's entirely possible to believe *both* that the laws of nature are always consistent *and* that God can intervene if he wants to.

Think about it. The law of gravity says that if I drop a marble, it will fall to the ground. But you might intervene and catch it before it hits the floor.

Similarly, God can intervene in the world and make unexpected things happen. If God is the Creator of everything, it does make sense that he can reach in and change the world when he chooses—making the impossible possible.

So, believing in miracles doesn't undermine a scientific understanding of how the world works. Christians would say that the laws of nature have been built into the universe by their Creator. And if we didn't know about the laws of nature, we wouldn't recognise a miracle when we saw one!

Miracles do need investigating, though. We don't just take them on trust. We ask questions and explore other possible explanations. That's what we're going to do in the next chapter with the most important miracle of all in the Christian faith: the resurrection of Jesus from the dead.

First of all, though, we need to think about another way in which the Bible's claims about things that have happened seem to contradict science.

In the Beginning

You might know that according to physicists, the universe is about 13.8 billion years old. Geologists think

that the earth is about 4,500 million years old. And evolutionary biologists tell us that all plants and animals, including humans, evolved from each other, starting with the earliest multi-celled life forms which appeared around 600 million years ago.

The first chapter of the Bible, in the book of Genesis, describes the development of the world in a different way. It talks about six days in which God created everything in the universe—including the sun, the moon, plants, birds, fish, land animals and finally two humans called Adam and Eve.

You can see why this has been a big source of conflict between science and religion. Don't those two accounts completely contradict each other?

Well… not necessarily.

Let's imagine you put five Christians in a room together. They're all intelligent people. They all think that it's very important to believe that what the Bible says is true—in fact, they're Bible experts. And they all also love science.

You might think that those five Christians would all come to the same conclusions about the beginning of the world and the origins of the human race. But the fact is, they all disagree!

One thinks that God created the world in six literal days of one Earth week—after all, that is what the text of the Bible says, and God is all-powerful. Maybe he decided to make the earth look older than it is for some reason, and that's why geologists think it is so old.

Another says, "Hold on a moment." The word "day" in Genesis is used with different meanings. So, the six days in Genesis could represent six ages of time. They weren't "days" in a literal sense. Each stage of the creation probably took several hundred million years, but it did happen in the order described in the Bible.

The third believes that the most important aspect of the Bible's account isn't actually what order things happened in or how long it took at all. There are bigger, wider truths that the Bible is communicating—like the sheer fact that God did the creating—and that's what this person focuses on.

Person number 4 argues that all the plants and animals on earth evolved from simple multi-celled organisms. This evolution didn't happen randomly but was guided by God. Then humans were created separately, starting with Adam and Eve.

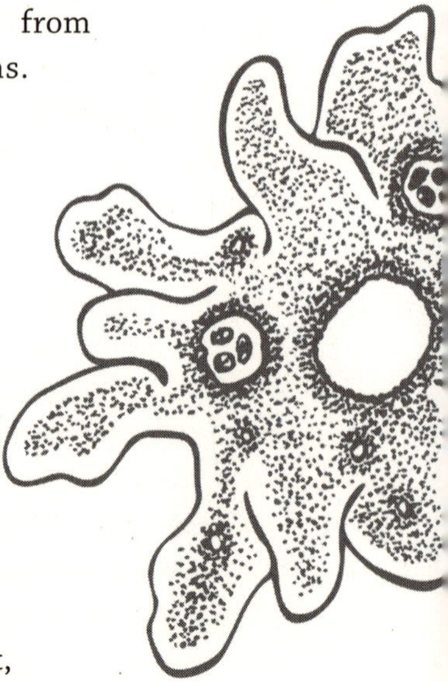

Person number 5 would say that evolution can explain some differences between species, but that every plant and animal on Earth did not evolve from one common ancestor. God created, for example, some sort of fish, a bird, some lizards, a type of rabbit, and so on, and then let evolution take its course from there.

And that's only five people!

I don't actually think all of those opinions are equally valid, but there's no need to go into the details right now. You can probably tell that if I tried to explain every single argument and debate, take you through all the evidence, and give you everything you need to form your own conclusions, it would take me a lot of pages.*

What You Can Be Sure Of

But that's okay, because you've already heard enough to be clear about some very important things.

Let's say that someone tells you that you can't believe in both God and evolution. You can be sure that they're incorrect: lots of evolutionary biologists believe in God, and many Christians will sign up to some form of evolution.

Or someone claims that all Christians believe that the earth is only 6,000 years old. You can tell them that this is not quite right; that is one interpretation of the Bible, yes, but it's not the only legitimate interpretation.

Or someone might tell you that the Bible's view of the origins of the world can never be compatible with science. You can say with confidence that it can. And there are a lot of big brains all over the world who are thinking through exactly how. (Maybe you'll become one of them.)

The most important thing to bear in mind is probably that the question of how exactly God created the world is *not core to Christian belief*. It is the idea that he did create the world that is central.

---

* I (John) have written a book on this called *Six Days That Divide the World*. My book *Cosmic Chemistry: Do God and Science Mix?* also looks at this topic.

Time for Some Evidence

We started this book asking whether science and faith in God mix. We talked about various ways in which they do—in fact, the pursuit of science may even make *more* sense if you believe in God than if you don't. We found out that science can't prove conclusively whether or not God exists, although many have found that the evidence of science is enough to convince them that he does.

We said that the Bible claims that there *is* a God—and we've considered a few aspects of the relationship between the Bible and science. We're now ready for the main event. What evidence *does* the Bible give us for the existence of God?

It's time to think about Jesus.

In Short

- The Bible describes miracles. These may seem like a contradiction of the laws of nature, but this isn't so: Christians believe that God can intervene and make what is impossible possible.
- If someone claims that a miracle has happened, that shouldn't just be taken on trust. It needs investigating.
- Some say that the Bible's account of creation contradicts science. Thoughtful Christians disagree on how the creation account should be interpreted, but we can be clear that science *can* fit together well with the idea that God created the world.

Chapter 7

A FIRST-CENTURY MYSTERY

The evidence for Jesus' resurrection

The most important person in the Christian faith is an ordinary-looking Jewish man called Jesus who lived in the Roman province of Judea in the first part of the 1st century AD.

The Bible says that Jesus was (and is) God. Jesus was the one who wrote the laws of nature. He was there at the beginning of time. He was then born as a human and lived for about 30 years, teaching people about God and performing miracles.

Science says that God *might* exist. The question for us is: could Jesus be that God?

A Mystery

Here are a few facts about Jesus stated by the Roman historian Tacitus (who was writing a few decades after Jesus and was definitely not a Christian).

Tacitus
c. 56– c. 120

- A man known as "Christus" (i.e. Jesus Christ) underwent the death penalty during the reign of the Roman emperor Tiberius.
- There was some sort of religious belief about Christus (presumably the belief that he was God, or the Son of God). This belief initially stopped spreading when he was executed.
- But soon afterwards, this belief spread very rapidly—not only in Judea, where Jesus came from, but even in Rome, the capital of the empire.*

It makes sense that after Jesus was killed, the belief that he was God seemed to flicker out. After all, how could God be put to death on a Roman cross?

But then we find ourselves face to face with a mystery. Belief in Jesus rose in popularity again very soon after his death. And it rose in popularity not just among Jewish people like Jesus himself but in the multicultural city of Rome.

---

* Tacitus, *Annals* 15.44.

Why would people who didn't even believe in God (at least, not in the God described in the Bible) suddenly decide that a dead man they'd never met was God? And in large numbers? It's extremely strange.

Fortunately, scientists like strange things! It's when we spot odd and surprising things that we seek out new explanations, formulate new theories and discover the truth.

So, why did so many people believe that Jesus was God, even after he'd died? The Bible's answer is that *Jesus didn't stay dead.* He rose again—proving once and for all that he is indeed the all-powerful, death-defeating Son of God. And after he rose again, he appeared to many followers, who then shared the news with others.

This is the explanation that we are going to put to the test in this chapter. Did Jesus really rise from the dead?

Exploring this question will lead us to understand why Christianity spread rapidly after Jesus died. But it will also help us to answer a bigger question: is it true that Jesus is God?

Blood and Water: Did Jesus Die?

If you're interested in human biology, you'll be interested in one of the details that the Bible gives about Jesus' death.

He was crucified. This means his hands and feet were nailed onto a large wooden cross, which was then stood up so that he hung high above the ground. After hours of pain, most prisoners being crucified would suffocate to death. It was grim.

Because the crosses were raised high up, it was not always easy to tell whether the prisoner had actually died or just fainted. But the Romans were wise to this. To check whether the person was dead, they took a long spear and shoved it up into the prisoner's side. This is exactly what they did with Jesus:

> *One of the soldiers pierced Jesus' side with a spear, bringing a sudden flow of blood and water.*
> *(John 19:34)*

Here's where biology comes in. What's the "blood and water" all about? Well, the water was in fact probably plasma, a clear liquid which forms part of blood. Normally plasma is mixed in with the rest of our blood, which is why we don't see it when we bleed. But after you die, it starts to separate.

The soldier wouldn't have known what plasma was. Nor would anyone who saw the "blood and water" flow out of Jesus' side. But they did know what it meant. Jesus was dead. Thoroughly, undeniably dead.

This is the first piece of the puzzle. You can't rise if you didn't die. But Jesus definitely died. The "blood and water" detail is just one piece of evidence that leads historians to be completely confident about this.

The Empty Tomb: Was Jesus Gone?

We can also be confident that two days after Jesus' body was placed in a tomb, that tomb was empty.

This is what the Bible tells us. But how can we be sure that it's true? Well, here's a comparison. Let's imagine for a moment that you have a mischief-making boy called Jackson in your class at school. Jackson wants to get you in trouble, so one day he goes up to your teacher and tells her that you haven't done your homework. Which is a lie.

What would you do? It wouldn't be hard to prove Jackson wrong, would it? All you'd need to do is get out your bag and produce your homework. "Here it is," you'd say to your teacher, and it'd be Jackson who'd find himself in detention instead of you.

Your homework is a bit like Jesus' dead body. (Stay with me on this...) Let's imagine that Jesus' followers were lying, just like Jackson. Jesus hadn't risen from the dead—his body was still in the tomb. If that was so, what would the Romans have done when Jesus' followers started to spread rumours that Jesus was alive? They'd just go straight to the tomb and produce the body. "Here it is," they'd say, and nobody would believe that Jesus had risen from the dead.

But that didn't happen. So, the tomb *must* have been empty.* Within two days after Jesus died, his body had disappeared. That is the theory that best fits the facts.

However, this doesn't prove that Jesus rose from the dead.

---

* The historian Michael Grant confirms this: "The evidence is firm and plausible enough to necessitate the conclusion that the tomb was, indeed, found empty." From *Jesus: An Historian's Review of the Gospels* (Charles Scribner & Sons, 1977), page 176.

Tomb Raiders: Did Jesus Rise?

A much more natural explanation for an empty tomb would be that somebody had secretly taken the body away. And that is exactly what was claimed by people at the time who *didn't* believe that Jesus was God. Here's another non-Christian account of the start of Christianity, written down in about AD 155:*

> *His disciples stole him by night from the tomb ... and they deceive men, saying that he is risen from the dead.*

Could this be true? Could Jesus' disciples have stolen the body and then lied about it?

One answer to that question is another question: why *would* they do that? Bear in mind that Paul (one of the writers of the Bible) wrote to some other believers, "If Christ has not been raised, your faith is futile".** Being a Christian makes absolutely no sense if you don't think that Jesus has really risen from the dead, because that's the key piece of evidence for Jesus being God. So, what would the disciples' motivation be for spreading the news that Jesus had risen, if they knew that that wasn't true?

Maybe they were just having a bit of fun, like your imaginary classmate Jackson? If that's true, it didn't stay fun for long. The Jewish authorities and the Romans had killed Jesus, and there was nothing to stop them from killing other troublemakers too. A man

---

* Justin Martyr, *The Dialogue with Trypho*, chapter 108. Translated by A. Lukyn Williams (SPCK, 1930).

** 1 Corinthians 15:17.

named Stephen is thought to have been the first of Jesus' followers to be brutally murdered, but he was soon followed by others.

Why were Jesus' followers willing to lose their lives in order to maintain the claim that Jesus had risen from the dead, if in fact they'd hidden his body somewhere?

Another possibility is that somebody *else* stole the body—a robber of some kind. This again raises the question: *why?* Jesus had died a criminal's death and was not buried with anything valuable. It was rich people's graves you'd steal from, not a grave like that. Plus, the Bible tells us that the Romans posted a guard on the tomb—so how would robbers have got in?

Even so, robbery may still seem like the best explanation for the empty tomb. And this is exactly what Mary Magdalene, one of the first people to see the empty tomb, assumed had happened:

> *"They have taken my Lord away," she said,*
> *"and I don't know where they have put him."*
> *(John 20:13)*

People don't just assume that someone has risen from the dead. And according to the Bible, Mary and the other disciples didn't do that either. They thought someone must have taken the body away.

So, what changed their mind? The answer is that they saw Jesus alive after he had died.

500 People: Was Jesus Seen?

The Bible includes a number of detailed stories in which the risen Jesus was seen by his followers over a period of 40 days. First of all by Mary, and then by Peter and many others. And not just seen—he hung out with some of them for several hours, walking, talking and eating. He even cooked them breakfast.*

The scholar Gerd Lüdemann (who is an atheist) argues that these appearances are the only thing that can explain the growth of the church in those early years. This is the only thing that can have given Jesus' followers the confidence to spread the news that he had risen. Lüdemann says:**

> It may be taken as historically certain that Peter and the disciples had experiences after Jesus' death in which Jesus appeared to them as the risen Christ.

However, Lüdemann is not a Christian! He thinks that these "appearances" were actually visions or hallucinations. The disciples did believe in them, but they weren't really real.

---

* Jesus meets the women at the tomb: Matthew 28:8-10; John 20:14-18. Jesus walks with two disciples: Luke 24:13-32. Jesus appears to many disciples: Luke 24:33-49; John 20:19-29. Jesus cooks breakfast: John 21:1-23.

** *What Really Happened to Jesus? A Historical Approach to the Resurrection*, translated by John Bowden (Westminster John Knox, 1995), page 80.

So... does that view hold water? Does this type of hallucination happen?

Psychologists would tell us that, yes, it's possible to have a vision of a friend who has died. Many people have had this experience—as many as 7% of those grieving a recent loss.* So Mary could have been hallucinating when she saw Jesus outside the empty tomb.

But what about 500 people seeing Jesus all at once? That claim was made by Paul in a letter written in AD 53 or 54 (so only 20 years or so after Jesus' death).** Paul made a point of saying that most of these 500 people were still alive—in other words, Paul's readers could go and check with them to see if his claim was true! So we can assume that 500 people really did see the risen Jesus—or at least they thought they had seen him.

But psychologists scratch their heads at this because there are no documented cases of large groups of people all having the same hallucination at once.*** It doesn't happen. Hallucinations might seem like a good theory, but the scientific evidence for them just isn't there.

Finally, you might be wondering if Jesus came back as a ghost. Well, Jesus asked his friend Thomas to

---

* André Aleman and Frank Larøi, *Hallucinations: The Science of Idiosyncratic Perception* (American Psychological Association, 2008), page 67.

** 1 Corinthians 15:6.

*** The New Testament scholar Mike Licona recounts that he emailed Frank Larøi, a psychologist and an author of the book *Hallucinations*, to ask why he hadn't included any mention of group hallucinations in the book. Larøi responded that he and his co-author had been unable to find any documented cases of group hallucinations. You can read about this here: "Appearances of Mary and Jesus' Resurrection Appearances: Weekly Q & A with Dr. William Lane Craig", *The Good Book* blog, 26th October, 2018: www.biola.edu/blogs/good-book-blog/2018/appearances-of-mary-and-jesus-resurrection-appearances touch him; he also ate a fish in front of his followers. Whatever you think of ghosts, you can agree that this is not very ghostly behaviour! Plus, people did believe in ghosts and spirits in the ancient world, but Jesus' friends didn't come to that conclusion about him. It's clear that they were convinced he was really alive. For them, there was only one explanation that made sense of all the evidence.

Why Christianity?

The existence of the Christian church is a fact. Very soon after Jesus died, the idea spread that he was alive again. And it spread quickly. People with different backgrounds, beliefs, languages, and statuses all believed that Jesus had risen from the dead and that this proved that he was God. People of every nation still believe this today.

And many Christians today would say that the resurrection is the main thing that proves that God exists at all. If Jesus rose from the dead, then everything he said about himself was true—and that includes the existence of God.

Whole books have been written about the evidence for the resurrection. This short chapter could not possibly say it all! But whether or not you are convinced yet, I would encourage you to keep exploring—because this really matters. If Jesus really did rise from the dead, it's life-changing.

In Short

- Many Christians would say that the reason why they believe in God is because they believe in Jesus.
- Historians tell us that Jesus definitely lived and died, and that many people believed he was God. In fact, this belief spread rapidly soon after Jesus' death.
- It's hard to explain this rapid spread of belief—why would you believe that a dead man was God? The most obvious explanation is that Jesus had risen from the dead. This is what the Bible claims.
- It's hard to explain away this claim. In particular, 500 people saw Jesus all at once after he died. It's not clear how this could have happened unless he was really there.

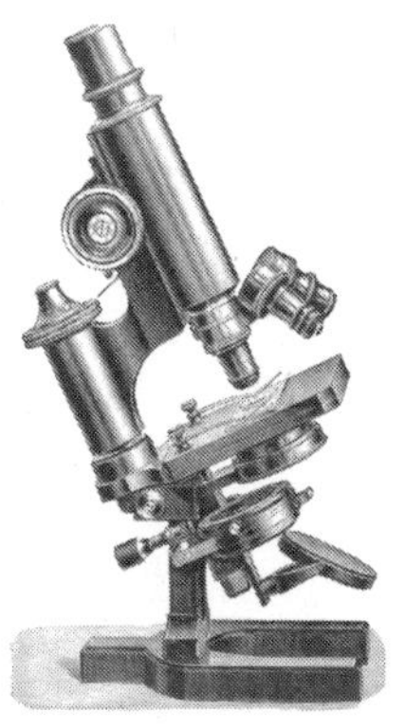

Chapter 8

ENTERING THE LAB

How to test it out yourself

You probably know that a big part of science is repeating experiments.

Let's say a range of medicines is being tested to see which is the best at treating a particular illness. You wouldn't just give the medicines to one person and see what happened. You'd give them to lots of people—preferably thousands of people. You need to know that Medicine A works better for all of them than Medicine B. If you only tested them on one person, it might be a fluke.

Or let's say an aircraft company is designing a new helicopter. The engineers have done their maths properly, and the mechanics have done their welding carefully, so, in theory, the helicopter should be good to go.

But aircraft companies don't just assume everything will be fine. They will test the helicopter in lots of different ways to make sure it works exactly as they hoped.

Science has to involve testing. And testing again. And testing again. Only then can we trust that a result is really true and reliable.

But how do you do that with Christianity?

Jesus' resurrection was a one-time-only event. Nobody is expecting it to happen again. We can consider the evidence for it pretty carefully, but we can't check it by repeating it.

In fact, some would say that Christianity isn't testable at all. Nobody alive today has ever seen Jesus. So how do we really know for sure that Jesus is alive and that he is God?

Fortunately, there *is* a way of testing the reliability of the Christian faith. And it has to do with people.

Christianity's Big Claim

You see, Christianity isn't just a set of things to believe. It's supposed to change your life.

To explain what this means, we need to pause the science for a moment and use another type of knowledge: theology, which literally means "the study of God".

In the final chapter of Luke's Gospel, one of the accounts of Jesus' life in the Bible, we read Jesus' own words to his followers, describing the basic message of Christianity:

> *This is what is written: the Messiah will suffer and rise from the dead on the third day...*

Jesus was using the words "the Messiah" to talk about himself. He suffered and rose from the dead. We've already covered that—it's the core belief in the Christian faith. But Jesus has more to add:

> *... and repentance for the forgiveness of sins will be preached in his name to all nations, beginning at Jerusalem. (Luke 24:46-47)*

It turns out that believing in Jesus' resurrection requires a response. Specifically, "repentance". That just means turning away from your old way of life, saying sorry to God for the things you've done wrong, and living God's way instead. And when you repent, you get "the forgiveness of sins".

This might sound quite far away from anything scientific, but bear with me.

The Bible says that humans are sinful—that is, we all rebel against God in one way or another. That makes us God's enemies, not his friends. And we can never be good enough to repair that relationship on our own. But this is why Jesus' death and resurrection are so crucial. The Bible says that *because of his resurrection, Jesus can bring us forgiveness and repair our relationship with God for us.*

This is the central claim of Christianity: because Jesus rose from the dead, you can have a personal relationship with God that you didn't have before. All you need to do is to repent and ask Jesus to be in charge of your life.

And this isn't a normal kind of relationship. However close you and your best friend might be, there'll still be times that you spend apart. That isn't the case with our relationship with God. Christians believe that God actually sends his Spirit to live inside us, *all the time.* God's Spirit changes us. The Bible even goes so far as to say that when the Spirit comes, it's like we've been born all over again. We've taken off our old self and put on a new self.*

That might all sound a bit complicated, and I'm aware that there are bits I haven't explained properly! But what it boils down to is this: *Christianity is supposed to change your life.*

And that is a claim you can test.

---

* John 3:3-8; Ephesians 4:20-24.

Testing, Testing

As I said, we can't run a scientific experiment that proves beyond doubt that Jesus rose again. We also can't take any measurements that check whether or not someone has been forgiven, and we can't detect any physical substances that confirm that God's Spirit is living inside someone. But all of us, whether we're scientists or not, are capable of looking at somebody's life and observing what it's like. And that's not a bad way of testing the truth of the Christian faith.

Maybe you know somebody who would say that they love Jesus and seek to follow him. What is that person like? Do you ever notice them acting differently to other people—maybe being more patient, or more truthful, or more peaceful? Would that person say that following Jesus has brought good things into their life—has changed them for the better? All those things would certainly describe the Christians I know.

Look at as many followers of Jesus as you can find—anyone who takes their faith seriously. Repeat the experiment. Find Christians of different ages, from different backgrounds, with different personality traits, and ask yourself (and ask them): what impact does being a Christian have in a person's life?

I suspect you'll find it's rather a lot.

The World We Want

Even having said all of that, I'm aware that Christians don't always fulfil the promise I've just outlined. Someone can go to church their whole life and still be grumpy and judgmental, or a bad parent, or a bit selfish. Christians throughout history have done bad things (like invading countries) as well as good things (like setting up orphanages, hospitals and food banks).

So although it is a good idea to test Christianity by looking at the changes in Christians' lives, we'll want to think about other sources of data too.

One question it's worth asking is: do Christian beliefs build a good society or a bad one?

An important German thinker called Karl Marx once wrote that faith in God is the "opium of the people" (or the "opium of the masses"). Opium is a drug that is sometimes used as a painkiller. It slows your body down and makes you sleepy. It also kills you if you have too much of it. So, in saying that religious belief is like opium, Marx was saying that although it might be pleasant in the short term, it is a seriously bad thing! In order to be truly happy, he argued, we need to get rid of it.

Karl Marx
1818–1883

Karl Marx's philosophy and writings—not just about God but about people, power, and how countries should be run—became the basis for a system of government called communism. For most of the 20th century, about a third of the world's population lived under communist governments. You might know that the result was *not* the increased happiness envisaged by Marx. These communist countries were led by dictators who controlled the lives of everyone else: Joseph Stalin, Chairman Mao and others. Millions of people starved.

The Polish writer Czesław Miłosz argued that it was in part the communists' belief in atheism that allowed this to happen. He wrote:*

> A true opium of the people is a belief in nothingness after death … thinking that for our betrayals, greed, cowardice, murders, we are not going to be judged.

In other words, if you don't believe in a God who cares about justice, it gives you permission to avoid taking responsibility for your own actions. And *that* is what's dangerous.

By contrast, the historian Tom Holland has argued that even though many people in today's Western societies are not Christians, the values that we hold dear are essentially Christian ones.** In particular, we think it's important to look after the weak and vulnerable—and that's an idea that comes from the Bible. The ancient Greeks and Romans did not think this was worth doing at all.

---

* He wrote this in the *New York Review of Books*, 19th November, 1998.

** His book about this is called *Dominion: The Making of the Western Mind* (Little, Brown, 2019).

So which is better? Christianity or atheism? Well, which world would you rather live in—a world in which people seek to put others first because they believe that is what God wants, or a world in which people believe that nothing we do really matters?

The Bible describes the earliest Christians as people who welcomed those who were different to themselves, shared their possessions, gave money to the needy and cared for those who were vulnerable. Not every Christian in history has lived up to that. But many have, and still do—because goodness, justice, mercy and peace are the goal the Bible sets for us.

The Personal Test

There's one more way of testing the truth of Christianity. The very best way. The way you can't do without if you're going to decide once and for all whether it could be true.

The very best way to test the truth of Christianity is to get to know Jesus.

After all, Christianity claims to be a relationship with a person, not just a set of opinions to sign up to. And you don't get to know someone by just learning facts about them. You have to spend time with them. Hear what they have to say. Understand what they're like. Experience how they act towards you.

And you can do that with Jesus.

You can't meet him face to face. But you can read his words. There are four accounts of Jesus' life in the Bible: they're called Matthew, Mark, Luke and John, named after the men who wrote them. Pick one of them and read it through. (Mark is the shortest, and it won't take you long.) Ask yourself: What is Jesus like? Do I like him? Can I trust him?

You could also try going to church. See what people say about Jesus there. (You'll find Christians to ask about how their lives have changed there too.) Ask yourself again: What is Jesus like? Do I like him? Can I trust him?

Only then can you really judge for yourself whether it's all true.

In Short

- Christianity isn't just a set of beliefs. It is supposed to change your life—giving you a relationship with the God who made the world.
- So, one way of testing out the truth of Christianity is to look at the lives of those who follow Jesus.
- Another way is to think about the world you want. Do Christian beliefs build a good society or a bad one?
- Finally, the very best way to test out Christianity is to look at Jesus: read an account of Jesus' life from the Bible and consider whether he could be someone you trust.

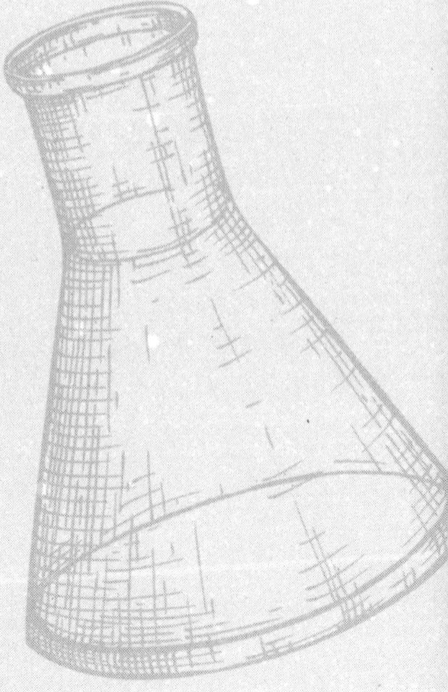

CONCLUSION

Science and God, together

In chapter 1, I mentioned that when I was a university student, I was told by a Nobel Prize–winning scientist to drop my Christian faith. He told me it would ruin my scientific career if I were a Christian.

My response to him on that day was this:

"Sir, what have you got to offer me that is better than what I have got?"

And he had no good answer.

Some people claim that the only way to know anything is through science. But for me, aged 19, science wasn't enough on its own. I needed a foundation for my life—one that gave me meaning and purpose. I had questions that science couldn't answer, and I believed I had found answers in Jesus. I didn't want to believe in something that science contradicted. But I also didn't want to believe *only* in science.

I'm 80 now. Over the past 60 years, I've found that my decision to stick with Christianity has proved to be right.

It didn't hamper my scientific career. Instead it gave me the motivation to pursue science—because I believed in a God who had created a world of order and who had designed my mind to want to make sense of that order and find out more about it.

But my Christian faith has also given me much more. It has given me purpose, meaning, joy and hope. It has been *better* than just science on its own. And it can be for you too.

Here's how the biologist Francis Collins put it:*

> As a believer who's also a scientist, science takes on a whole new wonderful kind of aspect, because you're exploring God's creation. When you discover something that no human knew before, God knew that. And you just got a little glimpse of God's mind.

The universe is amazing. Its designer is even more amazing! And he invites us to get to know him, both through the natural world and (best of all) through Jesus.

So here's my advice: be curious. Keep exploring. Who knows what you'll find out?

* He said this in an interview for CNN, 23rd December 2024. You can read it here: edition.cnn.com/2024/12/23/health/francis-collins-faith-science-public-health-wellness (accessed 7th April, 2025).

BIBLICAL | RELEVANT | ACCESSIBLE

At The Good Book Company we are dedicated to helping Christians and local churches grow. We believe that God's growth process always starts with hearing clearly what he has said to us through his timeless and flawless word—the Bible.

Ever since we opened our doors in 1991, we have been striving to produce resources that are biblical, relevant, and accessible. By God's grace, we have grown to become an international publisher, encouraging ordinary Christians of every age and stage and every background and denomination to live for Christ day by day and equipping churches to grow in their knowledge of God, their love for one another, and the effectiveness of their outreach.

Call one of our friendly team for a discussion of your needs or visit one of our local websites for more information on the resources and services we provide.

Your friends at The Good Book Company